TABLE
Of Contents

Text 1

Annotation Checklist

As you read the text, please annotate it using the following checklist:

- ☑ Underline any main ideas
- ☑ Circle any words you don't know
- ☑ Look up the words online
- ☑ Reread anything you don't understand
- ☑ Summarize after rereading
- ☑ Write Down things you find interesting

Note Taking

Name: _____

Date: _____

Mesopotamia: The Cradle of Civilization

Introduction

Have you ever wondered where and how the first cities began? Welcome to Mesopotamia, an ancient land with secrets waiting to be uncovered. Located in what we now call the Middle East, and nestled between the Tigris and Euphrates rivers, Mesopotamia is often called the "Cradle of Civilization." Thousands of years ago, before skyscrapers, the internet, or even electricity, this was where some of the world's first civilizations sprang to life!

History

Mesopotamia's fascinating story begins around 3500 BCE. Picture this: instead of one big country, the region was dotted with city-states like Uruk, Babylon, and Nineveh, each acting like a separate little country. Kings and queens ruled, and grand palaces and temples stood tall. It wasn't always peaceful, though. These city-states often fought for power and control, leading to many exciting stories and epic legends.

One such legend is of Gilgamesh, a mighty king who was the hero of one of the oldest known works of literature! Kings like Hammurabi also made a lasting impact, especially with his famous Hammurabi's Code, a set of laws so important that they were carved onto a massive stone pillar for all to see. These laws covered everything from trade and theft to injury and justice, showing us how advanced Mesopotamian society was.

Government

Mesopotamian governments were fascinating! Each city-state had its own ruler. The king wasn't just a political leader; he was also seen as a representative of the gods, making his role crucial both in the temples and in the palaces. This blend of religion and politics meant that the king had a pretty big job. He had to ensure the city was prosperous, the gods were worshipped properly, and that his people were safe and following the laws.

Assisting the king was a group of officials and advisors, helping manage everything from collecting taxes to maintaining city walls. Cities also had their own assemblies, comprising citizens who could offer advice and help make decisions. This form of early governance shows that even in ancient times, people understood the value of organization and leadership.

Religion

In Mesopotamia, life was deeply intertwined with religion. The Mesopotamians worshipped many gods, each in charge of different aspects of the world and human life. Enlil was the god of air, Enki of water and wisdom, and Inanna was the goddess of love and war. To honor these gods, the people built stunning temples called ziggurats. These weren't just places of worship; they were believed to be the home of the gods on Earth.

Priests played a crucial role, performing rituals to please the gods, interpreting omens, and even making sacrifices. The belief was that happy gods would mean a prosperous city with good harvests and victory in battles. Religion influenced many aspects of daily life and was a way for the people to understand and explain the wonders and mysteries of their world.

Food and Arts

Imagine living in Mesopotamia and sitting down for a meal. You wouldn't find fast food, but you'd have dishes made from barley, wheat, onions, beans, and meats like pork and mutton. People enjoyed fruits like apples, and for a sweet treat, they loved dates. Meals were often cooked in clay pots over open fires, and bread was a staple, baked in various shapes and sizes.

But Mesopotamians didn't just fill their stomachs; they filled their world with beauty too! They were masterful artists and craftsmen, creating stunning jewelry, pottery, and statues. They painted colorful murals on the walls of palaces and temples, telling stories of gods, kings, and daily life.

One of their most outstanding artistic achievements was the Ishtar Gate of Babylon – a massive gate decorated with blue glazed tiles and images of dragons and bulls. And let's not forget about their writing! Cuneiform, their system of writing, was used to record everything from epic tales like the "Epic of Gilgamesh" to daily business transactions. This writing was done on clay tablets, using a reed stylus — quite different from the pencils and keyboards we use today!

Daily Life

In Mesopotamia, not everyone lived in grand palaces. Ordinary people, like farmers, traders, and craftsmen, lived in smaller mud-brick houses. These hardworking folks were the backbone of Mesopotamian society, growing the crops, making the goods, and trading the products that kept the cities thriving.

Children had chores and, if lucky, schooling, but they also played with toys like clay dolls and miniature wagons. Education was mostly reserved for boys from wealthy families, where they learned reading, writing, and arithmetic, along with lessons on becoming scribes or officials.

Women in Mesopotamia typically managed the household but could also be priestesses, merchants, or even own property. Festivals and religious ceremonies were a big part of life too, with music, dancing, and feasts, offering everyone a break from their daily routines.

Fun Facts and Inventions

Mesopotamians were incredible inventors! They came up with the wheel, which revolutionized transportation and pottery making. The plow they created helped agriculture thrive by making it easier to till large fields. Their 60-second minute and 60-minute hour are a testament to their mathematical genius and are still used today!

They were also among the first to build boats for trade and travel, and their irrigation systems allowed them to grow crops in dry regions. Mesopotamian astronomers studied the stars and planets, laying the foundations for astrology and astronomy.

Another cool fact? They even had a goddess of brewing named Ninkasi, showing that they enjoyed a good drink and knew how to make it!

Reason for Decline

Like many great stories, Mesopotamia's also had an ending. Over centuries, the land faced many challenges. Continuous wars drained resources, and constant invasions by outside peoples like the Hittites and the Kassites weakened the cities.

Environmental factors played a role too. Over-irrigation led to soil becoming too salty for crops, and changes in the course of the rivers caused further agricultural problems. Slowly, as these issues mounted, the once-glorious cities of Mesopotamia lost their power and influence.

By the time of the arrival of Alexander the Great in 331 BCE, much of the splendor of these ancient cities had faded. Yet, the legacy of Mesopotamia lives on, influencing our world in countless ways, from our time-keeping and writing systems to fundamental concepts in law and government.

1 Which statement best summarizes how Mesopotamia is described in the introduction?

- a) Mesopotamia was a land full of modern technology and skyscrapers.
- b) Mesopotamia is known as the "Cradle of Civilization," located between the Tigris and Euphrates rivers.
- c) Mesopotamia was a single, large country in ancient times.
- d) Mesopotamia was mainly famous for its stories and legends.

2. What can be inferred about Mesopotamian city-states like Uruk, Babylon, and Nineveh?

- a) They were peaceful and seldom engaged in conflicts.
- b) They were unified under a single ruler.
- c) Each city-state functioned like a separate little country.
- d) They all shared the same laws and government structures.

3. Based on the text, Hammurabi's Code was important because it:

- a) Was the first set of laws ever written.
- b) Focused exclusively on trade and theft.
- c) Was carved on a massive stone pillar for all to see.
- d) Included only religious laws.

4. The author mentions "Mesopotamian governments were fascinating!" What evidence does the text provide to support this statement?

- a) The government was solely based on military power.
- b) Kings were seen as political leaders and representatives of the gods.
- c) Officials and advisors had no significant role in the government.
- d) The city assemblies comprised only of the king's family members.

5. What is the main idea of the section titled "Government"?

- a) The role of religion in Mesopotamian politics.
- b) The description of wars and conflicts in Mesopotamian city-states.
- c) How taxation was the most crucial part of Mesopotamian governance.
- d) The complexities of ruling each city-state and the responsibilities of a king.

6. Which of the following is a supporting detail about the daily life of ordinary people in Mesopotamia?
    - ○ a) They lived in grand palaces and had numerous servants.
    - ○ b) They played a vital role, being the backbone of society with their various occupations.
    - ○ c) Education was widespread among all classes.
    - ○ d) Ordinary people were involved in the construction of temples.

7. What does the word "epic" most likely mean in the context of "One such legend is of Gilgamesh, a mighty king who was the hero of one of the oldest known works of literature"?
    - ○ a) Long and adventurous
    - ○ b) Boring and uneventful
    - ○ c) Brief and insignificant
    - ○ d) Tragic and sorrowful

8. Who is primarily responsible for creating the art in Mesopotamia?
    - ○ a) The craftsmen and laborers.
    - ○ b) The astronomers and scholars.
    - ○ c) The kings and queens.
    - ○ d) The priests and religious leaders.

9. Describe how the Mesopotamian view of their gods influenced their architecture and daily practices.

_____

_____

_____

_____

_____

_____

10. Analyze how the environmental factors contributed to the decline of Mesopotamia.

_____

_____

_____

_____

_____

_____

11. Using evidence from the text, explain how Mesopotamian society was advanced for its time.

_____

_____

_____

_____

_____

_____

Write an essay discussing the influence of Mesopotamian inventions on modern life, using specific examples from the text.

_____
_____
_____
_____
_____
_____
_____
_____
_____
_____
_____
_____
_____
_____
_____
_____
_____
_____
_____
_____
_____
_____
_____
_____
_____
_____
_____
_____
_____
_____
_____

Answer key

1 Which statement best summarizes how Mesopotamia is described in the introduction?
- o a) Mesopotamia was a land full of modern technology and skyscrapers.
- o b) Mesopotamia is known as the "Cradle of Civilization," located between the Tigris and Euphrates rivers.
- o c) Mesopotamia was a single, large country in ancient times.
- o d) Mesopotamia was mainly famous for its stories and legends.

2. What can be inferred about Mesopotamian city-states like Uruk, Babylon, and Nineveh?
- o a) They were peaceful and seldom engaged in conflicts.
- o b) They were unified under a single ruler.
- o c) Each city-state functioned like a separate little country.
- o d) They all shared the same laws and government structures.

3. Based on the text, Hammurabi's Code was important because it:
- o a) Was the first set of laws ever written.
- o b) Focused exclusively on trade and theft.
- o c) Was carved on a massive stone pillar for all to see.
- o d) Included only religious laws.

4. The author mentions "Mesopotamian governments were fascinating!" What evidence does the text provide to support this statement?
- o a) The government was solely based on military power.
- o b) Kings were seen as political leaders and representatives of the gods.
- o c) Officials and advisors had no significant role in the government.
- o d) The city assemblies comprised only of the king's family members.

5. What is the main idea of the section titled "Government"?
- o a) The role of religion in Mesopotamian politics.
- o b) The description of wars and conflicts in Mesopotamian city-states.
- o c) How taxation was the most crucial part of Mesopotamian governance.
- o d) The complexities of ruling each city-state and the responsibilities of a king.

10

6. Which of the following is a supporting detail about the daily life of ordinary people in Mesopotamia?
    - ○ a) They lived in grand palaces and had numerous servants.
    - ○ b) They played a vital role, being the backbone of society with their various occupations.
    - ○ c) Education was widespread among all classes.
    - ○ d) Ordinary people were involved in the construction of temples.

7. What does the word "epic" most likely mean in the context of "One such legend is of Gilgamesh, a mighty king who was the hero of one of the oldest known works of literature"?
    - ○ a) Long and adventurous
    - ○ b) Boring and uneventful
    - ○ c) Brief and insignificant
    - ○ d) Tragic and sorrowful

8. Who is primarily responsible for creating the art in Mesopotamia?
    - ○ a) The craftsmen and laborers.
    - ○ b) The astronomers and scholars.
    - ○ c) The kings and queens.
    - ○ d) The priests and religious leaders.

Text 2

Annotation Checklist

As you read the text, please annotate it using the following checklist:

- ☑ Underline any main ideas
- ☑ Circle any words you don't know
- ☑ Look up the words online
- ☑ Reread anything you don't understand
- ☑ Summarize after rereading
- ☑ Write Down things you find interesting

yes!

Note Taking

Ancient Egypt: The Land of Pharaohs and Pyramids

Introduction
Imagine a land of towering pyramids, mighty pharaohs, and a river so important it was considered the source of all life. Welcome to Ancient Egypt, a civilization that flourished for over 3,000 years by the Nile River in northeastern Africa. It's a land full of mysteries and marvels, from the construction of colossal monuments to the intriguing process of mummification.

History
Ancient Egypt's history is usually divided into different periods, marked by the reigns of powerful pharaohs. It all started around 3100 BCE with the unification of Upper and Lower Egypt under the first pharaoh, Narmer. This event marked the beginning of the Pharaonic era and Egypt's journey as a unified, powerful civilization.

Through times of peace and conflict, prosperity and struggle, Egypt's story is woven into the fabric of its incredible monuments, detailed hieroglyphics, and profound cultural rituals. Key periods include the Old Kingdom, famous for the building of the Great Pyramids at Giza; the Middle Kingdom, known as a golden age of order and stability; and the New Kingdom, marked by mighty pharaohs like Ramses II and the famous Tutankhamun, whose tomb's discovery in 1922 stunned the world with its untouched treasure and incredible artistry.

Government
In Ancient Egypt, the pharaoh was more than just a king or queen; they were considered a god on earth, playing a vital role in maintaining the harmony and balance of the land. The pharaoh's word was law, and they had absolute power over the country and its people.

Helping the pharaoh run such a vast kingdom were high officials, priests, and nobles. The government was organized with various levels of administration, including a special class of scribes who recorded everything from tax collection to the recording of historical events. This hierarchy helped maintain order and ensure the smooth operation of the empire.

Religion

Religion was central to every aspect of Egyptian life. The Egyptians believed in a vast number of gods and goddesses, each responsible for different aspects of the cosmos and human existence. Major gods like Ra, the sun god; Isis, the goddess of magic and motherhood; and Osiris, the god of the afterlife, played crucial roles in Egyptian mythology.

Temples dotted the landscape, serving as places of worship and centers of the community. Priests conducted rituals to appease the gods and ensure the natural order of the world. The belief in an afterlife was also strong, leading to the practice of mummification and the building of elaborate tombs and pyramids designed to help the deceased in their journey to the next world.

Art and Architecture

The art and architecture of Ancient Egypt are among the most splendid and enduring in human history. The Egyptians excelled in creating breathtaking structures and artworks, many of which were meant to honor their gods and kings. The Pyramids of Giza, towering and precise, are among the most iconic symbols of this civilization's architectural genius. Built as tombs for pharaohs, these structures were constructed with such accuracy that they align with the stars and have lasted for thousands of years.

Art in Ancient Egypt was characterized by its highly stylized and symbolic nature, with paintings, sculpture, and carvings showing scenes of gods, goddesses, pharaohs, and everyday life. Artists used a rich palette of colors extracted from minerals to decorate tombs and temples. Hieroglyphics, a complex system of writing using symbols and pictures, were used not just for communication but as an art form, covering the walls of monuments and papyrus scrolls.

Daily Life

Daily life in Ancient Egypt varied depending on one's status and occupation. Most Egyptians were farmers, working the fertile lands alongside the Nile. Their lives were closely tied to the river, relying on its annual flooding to nourish their crops. Others were skilled craftsmen, priests, scribes, or soldiers.

Women in Ancient Egypt held more rights than in many other ancient civilizations. They could own property, run businesses, and were often involved in religious ceremonies. Children played games and toys, much like kids today, and attended school if they were boys from wealthy families, often training to become scribes or priests.

Science and Inventions

The Ancient Egyptians were not just builders of monuments; they were also brilliant scientists and inventors. Their understanding of mathematics enabled them to build pyramids and temples with astonishing precision. They developed a calendar based on the lunar and solar cycles, crucial for predicting the annual Nile floods.

In medicine, they were remarkably advanced, practicing surgery and dentistry and using various plants and herbs for treatments. The Edwin Smith Papyrus, an ancient medical text, provides insight into their medical knowledge, including diagnoses and treatments.

Reason for Decline

The decline of Ancient Egypt was gradual and caused by a combination of internal and external factors. Over time, the power of the pharaohs weakened due to political struggles, corruption, and civil unrest. Repeated invasions by foreign powers such as the Assyrians and Persians brought additional stress.

The final blow came with the conquests by Alexander the Great and later the Romans, ending thousands of years of pharaonic rule. Under Roman rule, Egyptian culture began to blend with Greco-Roman traditions, and the ancient religion slowly faded, especially after the spread of Christianity.

Despite its decline, the legacy of Ancient Egypt continues to awe and inspire people around the world. From monumental architecture and advancements in science to their intricate art and written language, the achievements of this ancient civilization remain a testament to human creativity and ingenuity.

1. Which event is noted as the start of Ancient Egypt's Pharaonic era?
    - a) The construction of the Pyramids at Giza.
    - b) The reign of Ramses II.
    - c) The unification of Upper and Lower Egypt by Narmer around 3100 BCE.
    - d) The discovery of Tutankhamun's tomb in 1922.
2. What is the main idea of the "Government" section?
    - a) The various levels of Ancient Egypt's administration and bureaucracy.
    - b) The pharaoh's role as both a god and a monarch in Ancient Egypt.
    - c) The educational system in Ancient Egypt.
    - d) The conflict and struggle for power within the Egyptian government.
3. What does the term "hieroglyphics" most likely refer to in the text?
    - a) A type of Egyptian sculpture.
    - b) A religious ritual in Egyptian temples.
    - c) An ancient form of Egyptian writing using symbols and pictures.
    - d) The architectural design of pyramids.
4. Based on the text, who primarily used hieroglyphics in Ancient Egypt?
    - a) Farmers and craftsmen.
    - b) Women and children.
    - c) Scribes and priests.
    - d) Soldiers and builders.
5. What can be inferred about the social structure of Ancient Egypt?
    - a) Everyone had equal rights and status.
    - b) There were clear distinctions in roles and status among different groups.
    - c) The society was predominantly matriarchal.
    - d) Craftsmen held the highest position in society.
6. Which statement supports the idea that religion played a central role in Ancient Egyptian life?
    - a) Priests conducted rituals in temples.
    - b) Women in Ancient Egypt could own property.
    - c) The Edwin Smith Papyrus was a medical text.
    - d) Art in Ancient Egypt was highly stylized and symbolic.

7. Which factor contributed to the decline of Ancient Egypt?
   - ○ a) The unification of Upper and Lower Egypt.
   - ○ b) The construction of the Great Pyramids.
   - ○ c) Repeated invasions by foreign powers and internal struggles.
   - ○ d) The development of the Egyptian calendar.
8. In the context of Ancient Egyptian government, a "scribe" primarily refers to someone who:
   - ○ a) Recorded historical events and tax collections.
   - ○ b) Built monuments and pyramids.
   - ○ c) Performed religious ceremonies.
   - ○ d) Governed the provinces of Egypt.
9. The "Old Kingdom" in Ancient Egypt is best known for:
   - ○ a) The unification of Upper and Lower Egypt.
   - ○ b) The building of the Great Pyramids at Giza.
   - ○ c) The invasion by Alexander the Great.
   - ○ d) The discovery of Tutankhamun's tomb.
10. True or False: Women in Ancient Egypt could own property and run businesses.
   - True
   - False
11. True or False: Hieroglyphics were used only for religious texts and had no artistic value.
   - True
   - False

12. What scientific accomplishments were the Ancient Egyptians known for?

_____

_____

_____

_____

_____

_____

13. How did the belief in an afterlife influence Egyptian art and architecture?

_____

_____

_____

_____

_____

_____

Examine how Ancient Egyptian beliefs about gods, the afterlife, and the natural world influenced their daily life, cultural practices, and artistic expressions. Discuss examples from government, religion, art, and architecture to illustrate your points.

_____
_____
_____
_____
_____
_____
_____
_____
_____
_____
_____
_____
_____
_____
_____
_____
_____
_____
_____
_____
_____
_____
_____
_____
_____
_____
_____
_____
_____
_____

Answer key

1. Which event is noted as the start of Ancient Egypt's Pharaonic era?
   - a) The construction of the Pyramids at Giza.
   - b) The reign of Ramses II.
   - c) The unification of Upper and Lower Egypt by Narmer around 3100 BCE.
   - d) The discovery of Tutankhamun's tomb in 1922.
2. What is the main idea of the "Government" section?
   - a) The various levels of Ancient Egypt's administration and bureaucracy.
   - b) The pharaoh's role as both a god and a monarch in Ancient Egypt.
   - c) The educational system in Ancient Egypt.
   - d) The conflict and struggle for power within the Egyptian government.
3. What does the term "hieroglyphics" most likely refer to in the text?
   - a) A type of Egyptian sculpture.
   - b) A religious ritual in Egyptian temples.
   - c) An ancient form of Egyptian writing using symbols and pictures.
   - d) The architectural design of pyramids.
4. Based on the text, who primarily used hieroglyphics in Ancient Egypt?
   - a) Farmers and craftsmen.
   - b) Women and children.
   - c) Scribes and priests.
   - d) Soldiers and builders.
5. What can be inferred about the social structure of Ancient Egypt?
   - a) Everyone had equal rights and status.
   - b) There were clear distinctions in roles and status among different groups.
   - c) The society was predominantly matriarchal.
   - d) Craftsmen held the highest position in society.
6. Which statement supports the idea that religion played a central role in Ancient Egyptian life?
   - a) Priests conducted rituals in temples.
   - b) Women in Ancient Egypt could own property.
   - c) The Edwin Smith Papyrus was a medical text.
   - d) Art in Ancient Egypt was highly stylized and symbolic.

7. Which factor contributed to the decline of Ancient Egypt?
    - a) The unification of Upper and Lower Egypt.
    - b) The construction of the Great Pyramids.
    - c) <u>Repeated invasions by foreign powers and internal struggles.</u>
    - d) The development of the Egyptian calendar.
8. In the context of Ancient Egyptian government, a "scribe" primarily refers to someone who:
    - a) <u>Recorded historical events and tax collections.</u>
    - b) Built monuments and pyramids.
    - c) Performed religious ceremonies.
    - d) Governed the provinces of Egypt.
9. The "Old Kingdom" in Ancient Egypt is best known for:
    - a) The unification of Upper and Lower Egypt.
    - b) <u>The building of the Great Pyramids at Giza.</u>
    - c) The invasion by Alexander the Great.
    - d) The discovery of Tutankhamun's tomb.
10. True or False: Women in Ancient Egypt could own property and run businesses.
    - <u>True</u>
    - False
11. True or False: Hieroglyphics were used only for religious texts and had no artistic value.
    - True
    - <u>False</u>

Text 3

Annotation Checklist

As you read the text, please annotate it using the following checklist:

- ☑ Underline any main ideas
- ☑ Circle any words you don't know
- ☑ Look up the words online
- ☑ Reread anything you don't understand
- ☑ Summarize after rereading
- ☑ Write Down things you find interesting

yes!

Note Taking

Ancient Greece: The Cradle of Western Civilization

Introduction

Imagine a world of mighty heroes, ancient gods, and beautiful cities, where ideas about democracy, philosophy, and art flourished. This was Ancient Greece, a civilization that arose over 2,500 years ago but still influences our lives today. Ancient Greece wasn't a single country like Greece is now, but a collection of independent city-states, each with its own way of doing things but sharing a common language and culture.

History

Ancient Greece's history is often divided into several periods, each with its unique developments and achievements. The Minoan and Mycenaean civilizations laid early foundations, but it's the Classical Period, especially in cities like Athens and Sparta, that many remember best. During this time, the Greeks achieved remarkable feats in philosophy, art, and politics.

Famous historical figures like the philosophers Plato and Aristotle, the general Alexander the Great, and the statesman Pericles all came from this era. Greek mythology, filled with gods, goddesses, and epic tales like those of Hercules and the Odyssey, also played a significant role in Greek culture and identity.

Government

Each Greek city-state, or polis, had its own government and way of doing things. Athens is famed for developing democracy, where citizens could vote and participate in decision-making. In contrast, Sparta was known for its strict military regime and oligarchic rule.

These city-states were often at odds with each other, leading to famous conflicts like the Peloponnesian War between Athens and Sparta. Despite their differences, they shared a sense of Greek identity, especially evident when facing common enemies, such as during the Persian Wars.

Religion

Religion in Ancient Greece was polytheistic, with a pantheon of gods and goddesses who were believed to control different aspects of life and nature. Major gods included Zeus, the king of the gods; Athena, the goddess of wisdom; and Apollo, the god of the sun and music. The Greeks built magnificent temples for their gods, like the Parthenon in Athens dedicated to Athena.

Religious festivals, such as the Olympic Games, originally held in honor of Zeus, were crucial parts of Greek life, blending athletic competitions, cultural celebrations, and religious observances. Oracles, like the famous Oracle of Delphi, played a significant role in decision-making, from personal advice to matters of state.

Daily Life and Education

Life in Ancient Greece varied from city-state to city-state, but there were common elements. Men, especially in Athens, spent their days in politics, philosophy discussions, or attending the gymnasium. Women, primarily responsible for managing the household, had limited rights and were expected to raise children and maintain the home.

In terms of education, only boys from wealthy families received formal schooling, which included learning to read and write, studying works of literature like Homer's epics, and physical training for military service. Spartan education was notoriously harsh, focusing on discipline, endurance, and combat skills to produce strong warriors.

Arts and Culture

The Greeks made spectacular contributions to arts and architecture. Their ideals of beauty and harmony are seen in their statues, pottery, and buildings. Classic Greek architectural features like columns and pediments originated during this time and continue to influence modern designs.

Greek theatre was another crucial aspect of culture, with playwrights like Sophocles, Euripides, and Aristophanes crafting dramas and comedies that explored complex themes of human life and morality. These plays were performed during festivals and were an integral part of civic life.

Science and Achievements

Ancient Greeks were pioneers in science, philosophy, and mathematics. Philosophers like Socrates, Plato, and Aristotle laid the foundations of Western philosophy, questioning the world and human existence. In science, figures like Archimedes and Hippocrates made groundbreaking contributions in fields like physics and medicine.

Mathematicians such as Euclid and Pythagoras explored geometry and numerical theories, some of which form the basis of modern mathematics. In astronomy, Greeks like Aristarchus proposed early ideas about the solar system's structure, and Ptolemy later developed a geocentric model of the universe.

Reason for Decline

The decline of Ancient Greece was gradual and complex. Constant warfare, especially the Peloponnesian War, weakened the Greek city-states, making them vulnerable to external powers. The rise of Macedonia under Philip II and his son, Alexander the Great, eventually brought Greece under Macedonian control.

After Alexander's death, his empire fractured, and Greek power further diminished. The final blow came with the Roman conquest of Greece in 146 BCE. Although Greece became a part of the Roman Empire, the Greek cultural and intellectual heritage continued to influence Roman culture and, through it, the Western world.

Despite the end of Ancient Greece as a political force, its philosophical, cultural, and scientific ideas have left an indelible mark on history, shaping much of modern thought and civilization.

1 What was the primary form of government in Sparta?
- A) Democracy
- B) Monarchy
- C) Oligarchy
- D) Theocracy

2. Which period is known for the achievements of Plato, Aristotle, and Alexander the Great?
- A) The Minoan Period
- B) The Mycenaean Period
- C) The Classical Period
- D) The Hellenistic Period

3. The Olympic Games in Ancient Greece were held in honor of which god?
- A) Zeus
- B) Apollo
- C) Athena
- D) Hercules

4. Which event marked the final end of Ancient Greek political power?
- A) The Peloponnesian War
- B) The death of Alexander the Great
- C) The rise of Macedonia under Philip II
- D) The Roman conquest in 146 BCE

5. What is the main idea of the passage?
- A) The influence of Ancient Greek culture on modern civilization
- B) The history of the Greek pantheon and mythology
- C) The educational systems of Ancient Greek city-states

6. Which detail supports the idea that Greek city-states had different forms of government?
- A) Athens is famed for developing democracy.
- B) Sparta focused on military and combat training.
- C) The Greeks built temples like the Parthenon.
- D) Greek plays often explored themes of human life and morality.

7. In the context of the passage, what does the word "polis" mean?
- A) A religious temple
- B) A form of government
- C) A marketplace
- D) A city-state

8. According to the passage, who were responsible for laying the foundations of Western philosophy?
- A) Socrates, Plato, and Aristotle
- B) Sophocles, Euripides, and Aristophanes
- C) Zeus, Athena, and Apollo
- D) Archimedes and Hippocrates

9. How did the Oracle of Delphi influence Ancient Greek life?

_____
_____
_____
_____
_____
_____

10. Explain how the Peloponnesian War contributed to the decline of Ancient Greece.

_____
_____
_____
_____
_____
_____

11. Describe the role of religion in the daily life of Ancient Greeks.

_____
_____
_____
_____
_____
_____

Compare and contrast the governments of Ancient Greece city states with one other from the text. Be sure to give examples of how they are different or similar.

_____

_____

_____

_____

_____

_____

_____

_____

_____

_____

_____

_____

_____

_____

_____

_____

_____

_____

_____

_____

_____

_____

_____

_____

_____

_____

_____

Answer key

1 What was the primary form of government in Sparta?
- A) Democracy
- B) Monarchy
- C) Oligarchy
- D) Theocracy

2. Which period is known for the achievements of Plato, Aristotle, and Alexander the Great?
- A) The Minoan Period
- B) The Mycenaean Period
- C) The Classical Period
- D) The Hellenistic Period

3. The Olympic Games in Ancient Greece were held in honor of which god?
- A) Zeus
- B) Apollo
- C) Athena
- D) Hercules

4. Which event marked the final end of Ancient Greek political power?
- A) The Peloponnesian War
- B) The death of Alexander the Great
- C) The rise of Macedonia under Philip II
- D) The Roman conquest in 146 BCE

5. What is the main idea of the passage?
- A) The influence of Ancient Greek culture on modern civilization
- B) The history of the Greek pantheon and mythology
- C) The educational systems of Ancient Greek city-states

6. Which detail supports the idea that Greek city-states had different forms of government?
- A) Athens is famed for developing democracy.
- B) Sparta focused on military and combat training.
- C) The Greeks built temples like the Parthenon.
- D) Greek plays often explored themes of human life and morality.

7. In the context of the passage, what does the word "polis" mean?
- A) A religious temple
- B) A form of government
- C) A marketplace
- D) A city-state

8. According to the passage, who were responsible for laying the foundations of Western philosophy?

- o <u>A) Socrates, Plato, and Aristotle</u>
- o B) Sophocles, Euripides, and Aristophanes
- o C) Zeus, Athena, and Apollo
- o D) Archimedes and Hippocrates

Text 4

Annotation Checklist

As you read the text, please annotate it using the following checklist:

- ☑ Underline any main ideas
- ☑ Circle any words you don't know
- ☑ Look up the words online
- ☑ Reread anything you don't understand
- ☑ Summarize after rereading
- ☑ Write Down things you find interesting

Note Taking

The Roman Empire: A Legacy of Power and Innovation

Introduction

When we think of the Roman Empire, images of mighty legions, grand monuments, and powerful emperors come to mind. Rome began as a small city and grew into a vast empire, stretching from the British Isles to the Middle East at its peak. This empire lasted for centuries, influencing language, law, culture, architecture, and government in ways that still resonate today.

History

The Roman Empire's history is marked by both triumph and tragedy, peace and war. It began with the founding of the city of Rome in 753 BCE, although the empire itself didn't start until 27 BCE, when Augustus Caesar became its first emperor after years of political turmoil and civil war.

The empire saw periods of tremendous growth and prosperity under rulers like Trajan and Hadrian. It was also marked by conflicts and power struggles, with infamous emperors like Nero and Caligula. The Pax Romana (Roman Peace), a period of relative peace and stability throughout the empire, lasted over 200 years, beginning with Augustus' reign.

Government

The government of the Roman Empire was a complex system with the emperor at its head. During the Republic era (before the empire), Rome was governed as a democracy, with elected officials and a Senate. However, as the empire expanded, the government became more autocratic, with the emperor holding supreme power.

Roman law was one of its most enduring legacies, laying the groundwork for many legal systems in the modern world. These laws regulated daily life, citizenship, property rights, and legal processes, reflecting the Romans' commitment to order and organization.

Religion

Religion in the Roman Empire was initially polytheistic, similar to Greek mythology, with gods like Jupiter (king of the gods), Mars (god of war), and Venus (goddess of love). The Romans also absorbed gods and religious practices from other cultures within their empire.

However, with the rise and spread of Christianity in the 1st and 2nd centuries AD, the religious landscape began to change significantly. Christianity, initially persecuted, was legalized by Emperor Constantine in 313 AD and later became the state religion under Theodosius I. This shift had a profound impact on the Roman Empire and the broader world.

Daily Life

Life in the Roman Empire varied greatly depending on one's social status, wealth, and whether they lived in a big city like Rome or in the countryside. Romans valued family life, education, and the arts. Wealthy Romans lived in large, comfortable houses, often lavishly decorated with paintings, sculptures, and intricate mosaics.

Common people, known as plebeians, typically lived in crowded, multi-story apartment buildings called insulae. These buildings were often cramped and lacked basic amenities. Food in Rome ranged from simple meals of bread, olives, and cheese for the poor, to extravagant feasts with exotic dishes for the rich.

Culture and Entertainment

The Romans made significant contributions to art and literature, with poets like Virgil, Ovid, and Horace playing pivotal roles in shaping Roman literature. Public entertainment was a crucial part of Roman life. People flocked to the Colosseum to watch gladiator fights, animal hunts, and mock naval battles. The Circus Maximus hosted thrilling chariot races, captivating thousands of spectators.

Theatre and public baths were also integral to social life, offering relaxation, entertainment, and a place to socialize. The Romans were known for their architectural prowess, with constructions like aqueducts, temples, and forums showcasing their engineering skills.

Science and Inventions

Roman contributions to engineering and science were significant, particularly in architecture and civil engineering. They built extensive road networks, aqueducts, and monumental buildings, many of which still stand today. Roman law, medicine, and military tactics also advanced during the empire, influencing subsequent generations.

Their military technology, including the development of the Roman legion, siege engines, and advanced weaponry, was crucial for both defense and expansion. Romans also excelled in public health, implementing medical practices and public facilities like baths and sewer systems that improved urban living conditions.

Reason for Decline

The decline of the Roman Empire was a complex process influenced by various factors. It became too large to manage effectively, facing constant threats from external invasions and internal strife. Economic troubles, overreliance on slave labor, and a series of weak and corrupt rulers contributed to the weakening of the empire.

The division of the empire into Eastern and Western halves in the late 3rd century AD further complicated governance and weakened centralized authority. The Western Roman Empire faced increasing pressure from barbarian invasions and finally fell in 476 AD to the Germanic king Odoacer.

The Eastern Roman Empire, known as the Byzantine Empire, continued for another thousand years, preserving and passing on Roman and Greek knowledge and traditions until its fall in 1453 AD.

1 What year is traditionally considered the beginning of the Roman Empire?
- a) 753 BCE
- b) 27 BCE
- c) 313 AD
- d) 476 AD

2. Who was the first emperor of the Roman Empire?
- a) Nero
- b) Augustus Caesar
- c) Constantine
- d) Trajan

3. Which of the following was a significant change in religion during the Roman Empire?
- a) The worship of Jupiter as the king of gods
- b) The transition from polytheism to Christianity
- c) The introduction of Greek gods into Roman culture
- d) The practice of emperor worship

4. Based on the text, which statement shows a cause-and-effect relationship in the Roman Empire's governance?
- a) As the empire expanded, the government became more democratic.
- b) The Pax Romana ended due to Nero's rule.
- c) Roman law laid the groundwork for many modern legal systems.
- d) The emperor held supreme power as the government shifted from a democracy to an autocracy.

5. What is the main idea of the section on "Culture and Entertainment"?
- a) Roman culture was heavily influenced by Greek traditions.
- b) Public entertainment, architecture, and arts were central aspects of Roman life.
- c) The Romans focused solely on literature and poetry for entertainment.
- d) Gladiator fights were the most significant aspect of Roman entertainment.

6. Which detail supports the fact that the Roman Empire was extensive and diverse?
- a) The empire had complex legal and military systems.
- b) The Romans were pioneers in science and engineering.
- c) Rome's empire stretched from the British Isles to the Middle East.
- d) The Colosseum was the primary site for public games and entertainment.

7 Whose writings are most representative of Roman literature?
- o a) Plato and Aristotle
- o b) Virgil, Ovid, and Horace
- o c) Homer
- o d) Socrates

8. Discuss how Christianity's rise and establishment as the state religion transformed the Roman Empire.

_____

_____

_____

_____

_____

_____

9. Explain how the division of the Roman Empire into Eastern and Western halves affected its governance and ultimate decline.

_____

_____

_____

_____

_____

_____

10. Describe how the daily life of a wealthy Roman citizen differed from that of a common plebeian.

_____

_____

_____

_____

_____

_____

Write an essay on how the engineering and architectural achievements of the Roman Empire contributed to its strength and longevity, citing specific examples from the text.

_____

_____

_____

_____

_____

_____

_____

_____

_____

_____

_____

_____

_____

_____

_____

_____

_____

_____

_____

_____

_____

_____

_____

_____

_____

_____

_____

_____

Answer key

1 What year is traditionally considered the beginning of the Roman Empire?
- a) 753 BCE
- b) 27 BCE
- c) 313 AD
- d) 476 AD

2. Who was the first emperor of the Roman Empire?
- a) Nero
- b) Augustus Caesar
- c) Constantine
- d) Trajan

3. Which of the following was a significant change in religion during the Roman Empire?
- a) The worship of Jupiter as the king of gods
- b) The transition from polytheism to Christianity
- c) The introduction of Greek gods into Roman culture
- d) The practice of emperor worship

4. Based on the text, which statement shows a cause-and-effect relationship in the Roman Empire's governance?
- a) As the empire expanded, the government became more democratic.
- b) The Pax Romana ended due to Nero's rule.
- c) Roman law laid the groundwork for many modern legal systems.
- d) The emperor held supreme power as the government shifted from a democracy to an autocracy.

5. What is the main idea of the section on "Culture and Entertainment"?
- a) Roman culture was heavily influenced by Greek traditions.
- b) Public entertainment, architecture, and arts were central aspects of Roman life.
- c) The Romans focused solely on literature and poetry for entertainment.
- d) Gladiator fights were the most significant aspect of Roman entertainment.

6. Which detail supports the fact that the Roman Empire was extensive and diverse?
- a) The empire had complex legal and military systems.
- b) The Romans were pioneers in science and engineering.
- c) Rome's empire stretched from the British Isles to the Middle East.
- d) The Colosseum was the primary site for public games and entertainment.

7 Whose writings are most representative of Roman literature?
- a) Plato and Aristotle
- b) Virgil, Ovid, and Horace
- c) Homer
- d) Socrates

Text 5

Annotation Checklist

As you read the text, please annotate it using the following checklist:

- ☑ **Underline any main ideas**
- ☑ **Circle any words you don't know**
- ☑ **Look up the words online**
- ☑ **Reread anything you don't understand**
- ☑ **Summarize after rereading**
- ☑ **Write Down things you find interesting**

yes!

Note Taking

The Inca Empire: The Power of the Andes

Introduction

High in the Andean mountains of South America flourished an empire of immense wealth and sophistication: the Inca Empire. Known as Tawantinsuyu, meaning "the land of the four quarters," the Inca civilization was remarkable for its vast territory, advanced agricultural practices, and stunning architectural feats like Machu Picchu.

History

The Inca Empire began around the early 13th century AD and rose to become the largest empire in pre-Columbian America. Its growth was rapid, expanding from the region of modern-day Peru to encompass parts of Ecuador, Bolivia, Argentina, Chile, and Colombia.

This expansion was due to the Incas' powerful military, strategic alliances, and efficient infrastructure, which included an extensive network of roads and bridges facilitating movement and communication. The height of the empire's power and reach was in the mid-15th century under the leadership of Pachacuti, who transformed the Inca state into a centrally organized empire.

Government

The Inca government was highly centralized and authoritative, with the Sapa Inca, the emperor, at the top as the absolute ruler. He was considered divine, a direct descendant of the sun god Inti. The empire was divided into quarters, each governed by an appointed official who reported directly to the emperor.

The Inca used a system of tax called mita, requiring labor from its subjects for public projects, such as building roads and temples. Despite the lack of a written language, they kept records using a system of knotted strings called quipus, which recorded information ranging from census data to military logistics.

Religion

Religion permeated every aspect of Inca life, deeply integrated into their understanding of nature and the cosmos. They worshipped a pantheon of gods with Inti, the sun god, being the most venerated. The Incas believed their rulers were living gods, direct descendants of Inti, which legitimized the Sapa Inca's rule.

Rituals and ceremonies were crucial in Inca religion, often involving offerings to the gods to ensure good harvests, health, and victory in battle. The Incas also practiced mummification and ancestor worship, and they built impressive temples and shrines throughout their empire.

Daily Life

The Incas lived in a society where the community was paramount, and the concept of collective well-being, known as ayllu, was the foundation of their daily life. People worked the land together and shared the harvests. Men were primarily involved in agriculture, herding, and construction, while women were engaged in weaving, cooking, and child-rearing.

Homes were made from stone or adobe, with thatched roofs, and in rural areas, families lived in close proximity to their fields. In urban centers like Cusco, the capital, buildings were more elaborate, often constructed with finely cut stone that fit together without mortar.

Food and Agriculture

The Incas were exceptional farmers, cultivating a wide variety of crops such as potatoes, maize, quinoa, and tomatoes. They developed advanced agricultural techniques, including terracing and irrigation, to manage the harsh Andean environment.

Llamas and alpacas were important animals in Inca society, used as beasts of burden and for their wool. The Incas also had a varied diet that included meat from domesticated animals, wild game, and fish from the streams and coastline.

Arts and Technology

Incan art was expressed through textiles, pottery, goldsmithing, and architecture. Textiles were particularly valued, often used as a form of tax payment to the state. The Incas also developed metallurgical techniques to create beautiful objects from gold, silver, and copper.

Their most famous technological achievement was their architecture, characterized by the precise cutting and fitting of massive stone blocks. Sites like Machu Picchu and the fortress of Sacsayhuamán are testaments to their skill in stone working and construction.

Inca Achievements

The Incas built an extensive road network, the Qhapaq Ñan, which stretched over 25,000 miles and connected various parts of the empire. They also invented the quipu, a unique system of knotted strings used for record-keeping and communication.

Medicine was quite advanced; Inca surgeons performed successful skull surgeries and used herbal medicines to treat various illnesses. The Inca's understanding of their environment allowed them to thrive in high altitudes and to create sustainable cities in challenging terrain.

Reason for Decline

The decline of the Inca Empire was sudden and devastating, precipitated by the Spanish conquest led by Francisco Pizarro in the 1530s. The Incas were already weakened by a recent civil war between two competing heirs to the throne, Atahualpa and Huáscar, which made them vulnerable to external threats.

The Spanish, with their advanced weaponry, horses, and tactics, were able to capture Atahualpa, and despite receiving a vast ransom in gold, they executed him. The introduction of European diseases like smallpox to which the Incas had no immunity, further decimated the population.

The empire's sophisticated infrastructure and centralization, while strengths in times of stability, became liabilities in the chaos of conquest and collapse. By 1572, with the capture and execution of the last Inca emperor, Túpac Amaru, Spanish control was complete.

1 What was the primary purpose of the extensive network of roads and bridges built by the Incas?
- o A. To facilitate military conquests
- o B. To enhance agricultural efficiency
- o C. To promote movement and communication throughout the empire
- o D. To demonstrate architectural superiority

2. What does the term "Tawantinsuyu" refer to in the context of the Inca Empire?
- o A. The name of the emperor
- o B. The capital city of the empire
- o C. The land of the four quarters
- o D. The system of taxation

3. Which of the following was NOT mentioned as an aspect of daily life in the Inca Empire?
- o A. Weaving textiles
- o B. Stone quarrying
- o C. Cooking and child-rearing
- o D. Agriculture and herding

4. Based on the text, which statement accurately reflects the role of religion in the Inca Empire?
- o A. Religion was a minor aspect of Inca life and was limited to the ruling class.
- o B. Inca religion was monotheistic, with Inti as the sole deity.
- o C. Religious practices involved offerings and ceremonies to please multiple gods.
- o D. The Inca rulers were considered to be ordinary humans without divine connections.

5. What is the main idea of the text about the Inca Empire?
- o A. The Inca Empire's decline was primarily due to the lack of advanced technology.
- o B. The Inca Empire was a sophisticated civilization known for its architecture, agriculture, and centralized government.
- o C. The primary achievement of the Inca Empire was its extensive road network.
- o D. Inca society was egalitarian with no social hierarchy.

6. Which detail from the text supports the importance of agriculture in the Inca Empire?
- o A. The Incas built roads and bridges to connect the empire.
- o B. The Incas worshipped a pantheon of gods, including Inti, the sun god.
- o C. The Incas developed terracing and irrigation to manage their environment.
- o D. The Incas created the quipu system for record-keeping.

7. In the text, the word 'mita' refers to:
- o A. A form of currency
- o B. A type of clothing
- o C. A system of taxation through labor
- o D. A religious ceremony

8. Who was considered to be the absolute ruler in the Inca Empire?
- o A. The Sapa Inca
- o B. Pachacuti
- o C. Francisco Pizarro
- o D. Inti

9. How did the concept of the Sapa Inca as a divine ruler benefit the Inca Empire?

_____

_____

_____

_____

_____

_____

10. Analyze how the centralization of the Inca Empire played a role in its decline after the Spanish conquest.

_____

_____

_____

_____

_____

_____

11. Describe the factors that led to the rapid expansion of the Inca Empire as mentioned in the text.

_____

_____

_____

_____

_____

_____

Discuss the significance of the Inca Empire's advancements in agriculture and how these contributed to the civilization's overall success and longevity. Include details from the text to support your discussion.

_____
_____
_____
_____
_____
_____
_____
_____
_____
_____
_____
_____
_____
_____
_____
_____
_____
_____
_____
_____
_____
_____
_____
_____
_____
_____
_____
_____
_____

Answer key

1 What was the primary purpose of the extensive network of roads and bridges built by the Incas?
- A. To facilitate military conquests
- B. To enhance agricultural efficiency
- C. To promote movement and communication throughout the empire
- D. To demonstrate architectural superiority

2. What does the term "Tawantinsuyu" refer to in the context of the Inca Empire?
- A. The name of the emperor
- B. The capital city of the empire
- C. The land of the four quarters
- D. The system of taxation

3. Which of the following was NOT mentioned as an aspect of daily life in the Inca Empire?
- A. Weaving textiles
- B. Stone quarrying
- C. Cooking and child-rearing
- D. Agriculture and herding

4. Based on the text, which statement accurately reflects the role of religion in the Inca Empire?
- A. Religion was a minor aspect of Inca life and was limited to the ruling class.
- B. Inca religion was monotheistic, with Inti as the sole deity.
- C. Religious practices involved offerings and ceremonies to please multiple gods.
- D. The Inca rulers were considered to be ordinary humans without divine connections.

5. What is the main idea of the text about the Inca Empire?
- A. The Inca Empire's decline was primarily due to the lack of advanced technology.
- B. The Inca Empire was a sophisticated civilization known for its architecture, agriculture, and centralized government.
- C. The primary achievement of the Inca Empire was its extensive road network.
- D. Inca society was egalitarian with no social hierarchy.

6. Which detail from the text supports the importance of agriculture in the Inca Empire?
   - o A. The Incas built roads and bridges to connect the empire.
   - o B. The Incas worshipped a pantheon of gods, including Inti, the sun god.
   - o C. The Incas developed terracing and irrigation to manage their environment.
   - o D. The Incas created the quipu system for record-keeping.
7. In the text, the word 'mita' refers to:
   - o A. A form of currency
   - o B. A type of clothing
   - o C. A system of taxation through labor
   - o D. A religious ceremony
8. Who was considered to be the absolute ruler in the Inca Empire?
   - o A. The Sapa Inca
   - o B. Pachacuti
   - o C. Francisco Pizarro
   - o D. Inti

Text 6

Annotation Checklist

As you read the text, please annotate it using the following checklist:

- ☑ Underline any main ideas
- ☑ Circle any words you don't know
- ☑ Look up the words online
- ☑ Reread anything you don't understand
- ☑ Summarize after rereading
- ☑ Write Down things you find interesting

yes!

Note Taking

Ancient China: A Tapestry of Tradition and Power

Introduction

Ancient China, known for its enduring history, vast territories, and profound cultural influence, was a cradle of civilization with its roots stretching back more than 4,000 years. This civilization developed along the fertile lands of the Yellow River, earning it the nickname "the Middle Kingdom." It is a land of innovation, philosophy, and imperial grandeur, giving rise to great dynasties, each leaving a unique imprint on history.

History

The story of ancient China is marked by dynastic cycles, periods of unity and disarray, and remarkable advancements. The earliest recorded dynasty is the Xia, though it is the Shang dynasty, with its bronze works and oracle bones, that provides the first archaeological evidence of Chinese civilization.

The Zhou dynasty followed, a time of great intellectual ferment that produced Confucianism and Taoism. The subsequent Qin dynasty, short-lived yet impactful, unified China for the first time under Emperor Qin Shi Huang. He standardized coins, weights, measures, and even the writing system, and began the construction of the Great Wall.

The Han dynasty succeeded the Qin and is often compared to the Roman Empire for its power, achievements, and longevity. It expanded China's borders, developed the Silk Road, and witnessed a flourishing of culture and technology.

Government

Ancient Chinese government was characterized by a central monarchy, supported by a complex bureaucracy. The emperor was considered the "Son of Heaven," with a divine right to rule. The bureaucracy was staffed by officials, often selected through imperial examinations based on Confucian texts, a system that emphasized merit over birthright, though it was not fully implemented until later dynasties.

The land was divided into provinces and counties, each with its own governor or magistrate, all answering to the central government. This hierarchical structure enabled the rulers to manage vast territories effectively.

Religion

The spiritual life of ancient China was diverse, with ancestor worship being fundamental to Chinese culture. The belief that the spirits of ancestors could influence the fortunes of the living made ritual and remembrance important practices.

Taoism and Confucianism were not just philosophies but also held deep spiritual significance. Confucianism emphasized ethics and proper behavior, while Taoism sought harmony with the Tao, the creative principle of the universe. Buddhism also arrived from India during the Han dynasty, adding to the rich spiritual landscape.

Daily Life

Daily life in ancient China varied greatly between the nobles and the peasants, but for most, it was centered around agriculture. The farmers lived in simple houses made of wood, mud, and straw, and worked the land, growing crops like rice, wheat, and millet. In their free time, they enjoyed games such as weiqi (go) and practiced martial arts.

Family was the cornerstone of Chinese society, and respect for elders was paramount. Education was valued, especially after the development of Confucianism, which taught the importance of moral virtues and social roles.

Arts and Culture

Art and culture in ancient China were expressions of the harmony and balance sought in Chinese philosophy. Poetry, painting, calligraphy, and music were held in high esteem. The Tang dynasty is especially known as a golden age of Chinese poetry with poets like Li Bai and Du Fu capturing the essence of both nature and human emotion.

Silk weaving, porcelain making, and jade carving were also highly developed art forms, revered both within China and coveted by outsiders, making them key exports along the Silk Road.

Food and Cuisine

Food in ancient China was not just sustenance but also an art form. The staple diet included rice in the south and wheat products like noodles and bread in the north. They practiced tea brewing and were the first to ferment and distill alcohol from rice.

Cuisine varied by region, with the imperial court enjoying the most diverse and luxurious food. Emperors hosted lavish banquets with delicacies from across the empire. Cooking was seen as an important skill, and soy sauce, vinegar, ginger, and garlic were commonly used to enhance flavors.

Science and Technology

China's contributions to science and technology are immense. They invented the four great inventions: papermaking, the compass, gunpowder, and printing. These innovations spread throughout the world and had a profound impact on global development.

They were skilled astronomers, charting the stars and planets with great accuracy and developing a calendar that was in use for centuries. In medicine, they practiced acupuncture and herbal healing, with an understanding of the body's qi, or vital energy.

Reason for Dynastic Changes

The cycle of dynastic change in ancient China was often due to internal strife, corruption, natural disasters, and peasant revolts. A dynasty might start strong, but as it weakened, it would be challenged and eventually overthrown, leading to a period of turmoil before a new dynasty emerged.

This cycle was philosophically underpinned by the Mandate of Heaven, a belief that Heaven granted the emperor the right to rule based on his ability to govern well and fairly. When a dynasty fell, it was believed to have lost this mandate due to its failings, thus justifying rebellion and the establishment of a new dynasty.

1 Which statement accurately describes the geography that influenced the development of Ancient China?
- o A. The civilization developed along the banks of the Nile River.
- o B. Ancient China was isolated from other civilizations by the Pacific Ocean.
- o C. The civilization developed along the fertile lands of the Yellow River.
- o D. Ancient China was primarily a desert landscape with little to no farming.

2. According to the text, what was the significance of the Zhou dynasty?
- o A. It was the first dynasty to unite China.
- o B. It produced the first archaeological evidence of Chinese civilization.
- o C. It was a time of great intellectual development, giving rise to Confucianism and Taoism.
- o D. It began the construction of the Great Wall of China.

3. Which dynasty is compared to the Roman Empire, and why?
- o A. The Shang dynasty, for its long-lasting bronze works.
- o B. The Qin dynasty, for its short but impactful rule.
- o C. The Han dynasty, for its power, achievements, and longevity.
- o D. The Xia dynasty, for being the earliest recorded.

4. What was the primary role of the emperor in ancient Chinese government?
- o A. To serve as the chief military officer.
- o B. To act as the "Son of Heaven" with divine rights to rule.
- o C. To work as a magistrate at the local level.
- o D. To be an official selected through imperial examinations.

5. What is the main idea of the text?
- o A. The text describes the various foods and cuisines of Ancient China.
- o B. The text outlines the history and cultural significance of Ancient China.
- o C. The text is a detailed account of the ancient Chinese dynastic cycle.
- o D. The text discusses the scientific achievements of Ancient China.

6. Which detail supports the idea that Ancient China was a land of innovation?
    - ○ A. The Tang dynasty was known for its poetry.
    - ○ B. The construction of the Great Wall began during the Qin dynasty.
    - ○ C. The bureaucracy was staffed by officials chosen through imperial examinations.
    - ○ D. China invented papermaking, the compass, gunpowder, and printing.
7. In the context of the text, what does 'ferment' most closely mean?
    - ○ A. To cause a public disturbance or unrest.
    - ○ B. To undergo a chemical breakdown of a substance by bacteria, yeasts, or other microorganisms.
    - ○ C. To develop in a gradual way, typically leading to a more complex form.
    - ○ D. To seethe with a particular feeling or state, often anger.

8 How does the text address the philosophical aspects of Ancient China?

_____

_____

_____

_____

_____

_____

9. What evidence does the text provide to show that China valued education?

_____

_____

_____

_____

_____

_____

10. What does the text suggest about the role of family in ancient Chinese society?

_____

_____

_____

_____

_____

_____

Discuss the significance of the dynastic cycle in ancient China and how it reflects the broader principles of Chinese philosophy and governance. Use evidence from the text to support your answer.

_____
_____
_____
_____
_____
_____
_____
_____
_____
_____
_____
_____
_____
_____
_____
_____
_____
_____
_____
_____
_____
_____
_____
_____
_____
_____
_____
_____
_____
_____
_____

Answer key

1 Which statement accurately describes the geography that influenced the development of Ancient China?
- A. The civilization developed along the banks of the Nile River.
- B. Ancient China was isolated from other civilizations by the Pacific Ocean.
- C. The civilization developed along the fertile lands of the Yellow River.
- D. Ancient China was primarily a desert landscape with little to no farming.

2. According to the text, what was the significance of the Zhou dynasty?
- A. It was the first dynasty to unite China.
- B. It produced the first archaeological evidence of Chinese civilization.
- C. It was a time of great intellectual development, giving rise to Confucianism and Taoism.
- D. It began the construction of the Great Wall of China.

3. Which dynasty is compared to the Roman Empire, and why?
- A. The Shang dynasty, for its long-lasting bronze works.
- B. The Qin dynasty, for its short but impactful rule.
- C. The Han dynasty, for its power, achievements, and longevity.
- D. The Xia dynasty, for being the earliest recorded.

4. What was the primary role of the emperor in ancient Chinese government?
- A. To serve as the chief military officer.
- B. To act as the "Son of Heaven" with divine rights to rule.
- C. To work as a magistrate at the local level.
- D. To be an official selected through imperial examinations.

5. What is the main idea of the text?
- A. The text describes the various foods and cuisines of Ancient China.
- B. The text outlines the history and cultural significance of Ancient China.
- C. The text is a detailed account of the ancient Chinese dynastic cycle.
- D. The text discusses the scientific achievements of Ancient China.

6. Which detail supports the idea that Ancient China was a land of innovation?
    - o A. The Tang dynasty was known for its poetry.
    - o B. The construction of the Great Wall began during the Qin dynasty.
    - o C. The bureaucracy was staffed by officials chosen through imperial examinations.
    - o D. China invented papermaking, the compass, gunpowder, and printing.
7. In the context of the text, what does 'ferment' most closely mean?
    - o A. To cause a public disturbance or unrest.
    - o B. To undergo a chemical breakdown of a substance by bacteria, yeasts, or other microorganisms.
    - o C. To develop in a gradual way, typically leading to a more complex form.
    - o D. To seethe with a particular feeling or state, often anger.

Text 7

Annotation Checklist

As you read the text, please annotate it using the following checklist:

- ☑ Underline any main ideas
- ☑ Circle any words you don't know
- ☑ Look up the words online
- ☑ Reread anything you don't understand
- ☑ Summarize after rereading
- ☑ Write Down things you find interesting

yes!

Note Taking

The Indus Valley Civilization: An Enigma of Antiquity

Introduction

Nestled along the fertile plains of the Indus River and its tributaries, the Indus Valley Civilization (IVC), also known as Harappan Civilization, emerged as one of humanity's first major urban centers. Flourishing from 3300 BCE to 1300 BCE, with its peak around 2600 BCE, this civilization is distinguished by its sophisticated city planning, advanced technology, and a script that remains one of history's tantalizing mysteries.

Unlike the contemporaneous civilizations of Egypt and Mesopotamia, the Indus Valley Civilization is not known through texts or chronicles; it is understood almost entirely through its material remains. Archeological marvels from this era, like the cities of Harappa and Mohenjo-Daro, showcase a standard of urban planning and civil engineering that stands out for its time.

History

The origins of the IVC are found in the Neolithic cultures of the region, which slowly transitioned into a Bronze Age society. By 2600 BCE, dozens of towns and cities were established, characterized by remarkable uniformity in city planning and architecture, indicative of an advanced understanding of urban design and strong central administration, or at least a shared cultural ethos that dictated town planning.

The meticulously laid out streets in a grid pattern, advanced drainage systems, and the uniformity of bricks used for construction across vast distances indicate a complex, interconnected civilization. There is evidence of social organization and labor division, with areas of the cities designated for specific industries, such as bead-making, metalworking, and pottery.

Evidence of contact with distant lands like Mesopotamia comes from Indus seals found in Sumer and vice versa, hinting at a vast trade network. Despite these external interactions, the Indus civilization retained distinct cultural characteristics.

Government and Social Structure

The precise nature of the IVC's political and administrative system is still a subject of debate. The systematic layout of cities and standardization across the region suggest some form of governance that implemented urban planning and controlled trade.

The absence of conspicuous palatial complexes or grand tombs suggests that power may not have been as centralized as in contemporary civilizations, or it may have been exercised in a less ostentatious manner. Alternatively, the significant buildings that have been interpreted as granaries could indicate that economic control was a source of power.

Houses were generally uniform in size and layout, indicating a more egalitarian society than was seen in other ancient civilizations. However, some larger structures suggest the existence of more affluent individuals or families.

Religion and Beliefs

Religious life in the Indus Valley is obscure due to the lack of decipherable religious texts. Yet, the artifacts unearthed, such as seals depicting various animal figures and a figure thought to be a proto-Shiva, suggest a pantheon that could have influenced later Hinduism.

Symbols found on several objects indicate a continuity of cultural motifs into the historical period of Indian culture. The prevalence of figures such as the Mother Goddess and the Pashupati seal lead scholars to speculate on the nature of their deities and rituals.

Large public baths, like the Great Bath at Mohenjo-Daro, are believed to have been used for ritual purification, a practice that is central in later Hinduism. The lack of grand temples, however, suggests either a religion without the need for monumental religious spaces or that the religious buildings were made of perishable materials and have not survived.

Daily Life and Culture

The daily life in the Indus Valley Civilization was marked by a level of sophistication unusual for its time. Most urban dwellers lived in sturdy brick houses, many with private wells, suggesting an emphasis on hygiene and convenience. The presence of individual bathing areas and elaborate city-wide sanitation systems reflects a culture that placed a high value on cleanliness.

The citizens of the Indus Valley were also fashion-conscious. Evidence from figurines and inscriptions suggests that both men and women wore a variety of garments and hairstyles. Cotton, known to have been cultivated in the region, was likely a popular choice for clothing due to its breathability in the hot climate.

Jewelry was a significant craft, as evidenced by the intricate beadwork and metallurgy. Gold and silver were fashioned into earrings, necklaces, and bangles, and semi-precious stones were carved into beads. This not only showcases their artistic flair but also suggests a society with class distinctions, at least in terms of wealth and access to luxury goods.

The urban centers were hubs of cultural activities. Although the Indus script remains undeciphered, the volume of seals and inscribed artifacts indicate a bureaucratic system likely involved in trade, taxation, or administration. The uniformity of weights and measures across a vast territory suggests a standardized system that facilitated commerce and trade.

Technological Innovations and Contributions
Technologically, the Indus Valley Civilization was remarkably ahead of its time. They were among the first to develop a system of standardized weights and measures, a necessary innovation for the complex trade networks they maintained. Craftsmanship in bead-making and metallurgy was sophisticated, with artifacts indicating a knowledge of alloy production, including bronze.

Agriculturally, they implemented advanced irrigation and water management systems to cultivate fields of wheat, barley, and possibly rice. Their granaries were among the largest structures in their cities, suggesting that food storage and possibly redistribution were crucial to their economic system.

Architecturally, their cities reflect a high degree of planning. Homes were uniformly constructed and laid out to adhere to city plans, indicating advanced knowledge in engineering and urban planning. The great bath of Mohenjo-Daro, with its waterproof lining and precise construction, stands as an emblem of their architectural and hydraulic ingenuity.

Reason for Decline

The disappearance of the Indus Valley Civilization is as complex as the culture itself. Climatic shifts are a leading theory, with evidence of a major drought occurring around the time the cities began to decline. This ecological disaster would have decimated agricultural production, leading to economic downfall and population dispersal.

There's also evidence of social and political change, possibly as a result of internal conflicts or shifts in power structures. The quality of urban planning and craftsmanship seems to deteriorate over time, hinting at possible social unrest or a breakdown in the shared values and norms that once unified the civilization.
Some suggest that the foreign migration into the subcontinent may have played a role, although this theory leans more on linguistic and cultural transition evidenced in Vedic texts rather than clear-cut archaeological findings of a violent conquest.

The decline of the Indus Valley Civilization was likely not a single event but a series of changes that collectively undermined the societal framework. As cities were abandoned, the knowledge and skills honed over centuries may have disseminated into rural areas, suggesting a transformation rather than an obliteration of the Indus culture.

1. Which of the following best summarizes the main idea of the introduction about the Indus Valley Civilization?
    o A) The IVC is understood through its advanced urban planning, despite no known texts.
    o B) The IVC was primarily an agricultural society.
    o C) The script of the IVC has been fully deciphered by historians.
    o D) The IVC had a complex political structure that was well-documented in texts.
2. Based on the information in the history section, what can be inferred about the cities of the IVC?
    o A) They were randomly planned with no particular uniformity.
    o B) They had little to no interaction with outside civilizations.
    o C) They exhibited uniformity in planning across different urban centers.
    o D) They were primarily rural with no significant urban development.
3. Which piece of evidence suggests that the IVC might have had trade relationships with distant lands?
    o A) The presence of urban planning.
    o B) The existence of uniform houses.
    o C) Indus seals found in Sumer.
    o D) The development of the script.
4. Which statement is supported by evidence in the text regarding the governance of the IVC?
    o A) The rulers lived in palatial complexes that were central to the cities.
    o B) The government may have controlled trade as a source of power.
    o C) There were grand temples which indicate religious governance.
    o D) The social structure was highly stratified with a clear ruling class.
5. What is the central idea of the passage concerning the religious beliefs of the IVC?
    o A) The IVC's religious texts are well-understood and indicate a polytheistic belief system.
    o B) The IVC had large temples for worship similar to other ancient civilizations.
    o C) The IVC's religious beliefs are largely unknown but are reflected in the artifacts found.
    o D) The IVC practiced monotheism, with the worship centered around a single deity.

6. Which detail from the text supports the idea that the Indus Valley people placed a high value on cleanliness?
   - ○ A) The existence of uniform houses across the cities.
   - ○ B) The sophisticated beadwork and jewelry.
   - ○ C) The presence of individual bathing areas and sanitation systems.
   - ○ D) The cultivation of cotton for clothing.

7. In the context of the text, what does the term "egalitarian" suggest about the IVC's society?
   - ○ A) It was a society based on extensive agriculture.
   - ○ B) It was a society where wealth was distributed evenly.
   - ○ C) It was a society that offered equal opportunities to all its members.
   - ○ D) It was a society where only the elite had access to resources.

8. What point of view does the author take when discussing the political structure of the IVC?
   - ○ A) Persuasive, arguing for a particular theory of governance.
   - ○ B) Informative, providing various interpretations without bias.
   - ○ C) Entertaining, focusing on the most dramatic aspects of governance.
   - ○ D) Critical, evaluating the failures of the political structure.

9. Based on the evidence in the text, what can you infer about the significance of technological advancements in the daily lives of people in the IVC?

_____

_____

_____

_____

_____

_____

10. Explain how the author uses artifacts and architectural evidence to make inferences about the religious practices of the IVC.

_____

_____

_____

_____

_____

_____

Imagine you lived in the IVC. Describe your daily life. Be sure to include your career, how you get food and water, and where you live.

_____

_____

_____

_____

_____

_____

_____

_____

_____

_____

_____

_____

_____

_____

_____

_____

_____

_____

_____

_____

_____

_____

_____

_____

_____

_____

_____

_____

Answer key

1. Which of the following best summarizes the main idea of the introduction about the Indus Valley Civilization?
   - A) The IVC is understood through its advanced urban planning, despite no known texts.
   - B) The IVC was primarily an agricultural society.
   - C) The script of the IVC has been fully deciphered by historians.
   - D) The IVC had a complex political structure that was well-documented in texts.
2. Based on the information in the history section, what can be inferred about the cities of the IVC?
   - A) They were randomly planned with no particular uniformity.
   - B) They had little to no interaction with outside civilizations.
   - C) They exhibited uniformity in planning across different urban centers.
   - D) They were primarily rural with no significant urban development.
3. Which piece of evidence suggests that the IVC might have had trade relationships with distant lands?
   - A) The presence of urban planning.
   - B) The existence of uniform houses.
   - C) Indus seals found in Sumer.
   - D) The development of the script.
4. Which statement is supported by evidence in the text regarding the governance of the IVC?
   - A) The rulers lived in palatial complexes that were central to the cities.
   - B) The government may have controlled trade as a source of power.
   - C) There were grand temples which indicate religious governance.
   - D) The social structure was highly stratified with a clear ruling class.
5. What is the central idea of the passage concerning the religious beliefs of the IVC?
   - A) The IVC's religious texts are well-understood and indicate a polytheistic belief system.
   - B) The IVC had large temples for worship similar to other ancient civilizations.
   - C) The IVC's religious beliefs are largely unknown but are reflected in the artifacts found.
   - D) The IVC practiced monotheism, with the worship centered around a single deity.

6. Which detail from the text supports the idea that the Indus Valley people placed a high value on cleanliness?
    - A) The existence of uniform houses across the cities.
    - B) The sophisticated beadwork and jewelry.
    - C) The presence of individual bathing areas and sanitation systems.
    - D) The cultivation of cotton for clothing.

7. In the context of the text, what does the term "egalitarian" suggest about the IVC's society?
    - A) It was a society based on extensive agriculture.
    - B) It was a society where wealth was distributed evenly.
    - C) It was a society that offered equal opportunities to all its members.
    - D) It was a society where only the elite had access to resources.

8. What point of view does the author take when discussing the political structure of the IVC?
    - A) Persuasive, arguing for a particular theory of governance.
    - B) Informative, providing various interpretations without bias.
    - C) Entertaining, focusing on the most dramatic aspects of governance.
    - D) Critical, evaluating the failures of the political structure.

Text 8

Annotation Checklist

As you read the text, please annotate it using the following checklist:

- ☑ Underline any main ideas
- ☑ Circle any words you don't know
- ☑ Look up the words online
- ☑ Reread anything you don't understand
- ☑ Summarize after rereading
- ☑ Write Down things you find interesting

yes!

Note Taking

The Mayan Civilization: Unveiling the Splendors

Introduction

The Mayan civilization conjures images of grand pyramids, majestic temples, and mysterious glyphs etched into stone—a testament to an advanced culture that has captivated the world. Nestled in the dense jungles of Central America, the Maya crafted one of the most intricate societies of ancient times. From their complex astronomical observations to their sudden and enigmatic decline, the Maya legacy continues to enthral scholars and laypeople alike.

Thriving for thousands of years, the Mayan people wove a tapestry of city-states each ruled by dynasties as divine as the gods they worshipped. Unlike the empires of the old world, the Maya were a collective of sovereign entities, connected by a shared cosmos of religious and cultural beliefs. It was a world where the boundaries between the supernatural and the mundane were blurred, and where time was not just measured but celebrated through a series of elaborate calendars.

History

In the shadow of colossal step-pyramids and beneath the canopy of celestial bodies, the history of the Maya unfolded. The Preclassic period bore witness to the burgeoning of civilization from small agrarian communities to sophisticated urban centers like Kaminaljuyu and Izapa. These nascent stages set the stage for an explosion of culture, commerce, and construction that would define the Classic period.

It was during the Classic period that the Maya reached the zenith of their cultural achievements. Cities like Tikal, with its towering Temple IV, and Palenque, with its exquisite Palace, became nerve centers of Mayan civilization. The Classic period is characterized by a flourishing of the arts, the erection of stelae that chronicled the deeds of the divine rulers, and a deepening of the intellectual pursuits that would see the Maya chart the heavens with unrivaled precision.

Yet, the Postclassic period brought with it winds of change. The majestic cities of the south fell into silence, and the torch of Mayan civilization was carried by cities in the northern Yucatán Peninsula. Here, at sites like Chichén Itzá, the influence of other Mesoamerican cultures, such as the Toltecs, is evident, demonstrating a period of vibrant cultural exchange and transformation.

Government

Mayan government was an elaborate hierarchy with the divine king—or "K'uhul Ajaw"—at the apex. These city-states were fiercely independent, often engaging in warfare, strategic marriages, and trade alliances to bolster their influence. Political life was a sophisticated dance of diplomacy and conflict, with power plays enacted through grandiose displays of wealth, ritual, and military prowess.

Beneath the king were ranks of nobles and officials, each responsible for various aspects of Mayan governance, from tax collection to the administration of justice. The influence of a city-state could often be measured by the expanse of its trade routes, which extended far beyond the Mayan heartland, bringing cacao, jade, obsidian, and quetzal feathers into the fold of their intricate economy.

Religion

Religion was not merely a facet of Mayan life; it was the foundation upon which their world was built. The Mayan pantheon was vast, with deities governing every element of existence—from the maize god, who personified the life-giving crop, to the rain god, Chaac, who wielded his lightning axe to bring nourishment to the earth.

Temples and pyramids were not just architectural feats but sacred spaces that bridged the earth and the divine. Within these stone walls, rituals of blood and incense ensured the favor of the gods. Priests, with their deep knowledge of astrology and the sacred calendars, held significant authority, guiding the rulers in matters of state and spirituality.

The religious calendar dictated the rhythm of Mayan life, with the Tzolk'in and the Haab' measuring out the spiritual and agricultural year, punctuated by ceremonies and festivals that bound the community together in reverence and celebration.

Daily Life and Social Structure

The daily life of the Mayans was characterized by a strong sense of community, with clear distinctions between the classes. At the top were the nobles and the priests, followed by the warriors, merchants, and artisans, and at the bottom were the peasants and slaves.

Most Mayans were farmers, cultivating maize, beans, squash, and chili peppers. These staple crops were the foundation of the Mayan diet, supplemented by hunting and fishing. The nobility enjoyed more varied diets, including chocolate, which was made from ground cacao seeds mixed with spices.

Artisans and craftsmen were highly valued for their skills in pottery, weaving, and carving. They created items not only for everyday use but also for ceremonial purposes. The vibrant Mayan markets were bustling centers of trade, where people bartered goods like salt, textiles, and jade.

The Maya lived in a range of environments from rural villages to large urban cities. Houses were typically constructed from a framework of wood or poles with thatched roofs and walls of mud or woven materials. In cities, the architecture was grander, with stone platforms supporting structures made of limestone and stucco.

Children were integral to the Mayan society, often learning their roles from their parents. Boys were trained in farming or craft, while girls were taught weaving and cooking. Education was more formal for the noble class, with instruction in writing, mathematics, and astronomy.

Arts, Food, and Inventions

Mayan art was deeply symbolic and intricately linked with religious beliefs. They excelled in the creation of stelae, murals, and sculptures that adorned their cities. The Mayans were also skilled weavers and potters, and their work often depicted gods, daily life, and significant historical events.

Their cuisine, based on the cultivation of corn, was enriched with beans, squash, avocados, and tomatoes. They developed ways to process corn via nixtamalization, which increased its nutritional value and allowed for the creation of various corn-based foods.

Among their significant inventions was the concept of zero in mathematics, which revolutionized their ability to calculate and maintain their elaborate calendar systems. They were also adept astronomers, predicting solar eclipses and the movements of celestial bodies with impressive accuracy.

Reason for Decline

The decline of the Mayan civilization is one of the great mysteries of history. Scholars propose numerous theories including overpopulation, environmental degradation, warfare, and political upheaval. Climate change, resulting in severe droughts, could have disrupted agriculture, leading to famine and social unrest.

Other researchers suggest that internal strife and warfare led to the fragmentation of their society. The competitive nature of the city-states, coupled with a reliance on a delicate ecological balance, may have made them vulnerable to a cascade of economic and social challenges.

The arrival of the Spanish in the 16th century marked the end of the Mayan civilization as it had existed for millennia. Though their cities fell into ruin, the descendants of the Maya continue to live in Central America, maintaining many aspects of their ancestors' culture and language.

1 What was the primary reason for the decline of the Mayan civilization according to the text?
- o A. Invasion by foreign powers
- o B. A series of natural disasters
- o C. Internal strife and warfare
- o D. All of the above

2. According to the text, which period of Mayan history is noted for the growth from small communities to urban centers?
- o A. Classic period
- o B. Preclassic period
- o C. Postclassic period
- o D. Colonial period

3. Which of the following best describes the Mayan government system?
- o A. A single unified empire
- o B. City-states ruled by divine dynasties
- o C. A divine king—or "K'uhul Ajaw" ruled the civilization with officials performaing tasks such as collecting taxes.
- o D. Rule by a council of priests and astronomers

4. Based on the text, which statement is false?
- o A. A. The Mayans developed a system of base twenty to calculate star patterns.
- o B. Temples and pyramids served as bridges between the earth and the divine.
- o C. Warfare was a common practice among Mayan city-states.
- o D. Mayan artisans were skilled in pottery and weaving.

5. What is the main idea of the second paragraph under the "History" section?
- o A. The Mayan civilization developed advanced astronomical systems.
- o B. B. The growth of the Mayan civilization.
- o C. Mayan city-states often engaged in warfare and political alliances.
- o D. The Mayan calendar was the most elaborate among ancient civilizations.

6. Which of the following is a supporting detail for the role of religion in Mayan life?
- o A. Priests had significant authority and influenced state matters.
- o B. Mayan farmers cultivated maize, beans, squash, and chili peppers.
- o C. The Mayans invented papermaking and the compass.
- o D. The Mayan government was a monarchy with a single ruler.

7. In the text, the word "zenith" most nearly means:
   - o A. Lowest point
   - o B. Middle stage
   - o C. Highest point
   - o D. Initial phase
8. Who is the author most likely to agree with regarding the interpretation of Mayan art?
   - o A. An archaeologist who sees it purely as decorative
   - o B. A historian who perceives it as a symbolic representation of their culture
   - o C. A biologist who studies the ecological influences on art
   - o D. An economist who focuses on the art's material value

9. How might the author of the text view the relationship between the Mayan religious and political structures?

_____

_____

_____

_____

_____

_____

10. What evidence from the text suggests that the Mayan city-states were both collaborative and competitive?

_____

_____

_____

_____

_____

_____

11. What details in the text support the theory that environmental factors played a role in the decline of the Mayan civilization?

_____

_____

_____

_____

_____

_____

Discuss how the Mayan civilization's advancements in various fields contributed to their society's complexity and their lasting legacy in history. Include examples from the text to support your discussion.

_____

_____

_____

_____

_____

_____

_____

_____

_____

_____

_____

_____

_____

_____

_____

_____

_____

_____

_____

_____

_____

_____

_____

_____

_____

_____

_____

_____

Answer key

1 What was the primary reason for the decline of the Mayan civilization according to the text?
- A. Invasion by foreign powers
- B. A series of natural disasters
- C. Internal strife and warfare
- D. All of the above

2. According to the text, which period of Mayan history is noted for the growth from small communities to urban centers?
- A. Classic period
- B. Preclassic period
- C. Postclassic period
- D. Colonial period

3. Which of the following best describes the Mayan government system?
- A. A single unified empire
- B. City-states ruled by divine dynasties
- C. A divine king—or "K'uhul Ajaw" ruled the civilization with officials performaing tasks such as collecting taxes.
- D. Rule by a council of priests and astronomers

4. Based on the text, which statement is false?
- A. The Mayans developed a system of base twenty to calculate star patterns.
- B. Temples and pyramids served as bridges between the earth and the divine.
- C. Warfare was a common practice among Mayan city-states.
- D. Mayan artisans were skilled in pottery and weaving.

5. What is the main idea of the second paragraph under the "History" section?
- A. The Mayan civilization developed advanced astronomical systems.
- B. The growth of the Mayan civilization.
- C. Mayan city-states often engaged in warfare and political alliances.
- D. The Mayan calendar was the most elaborate among ancient civilizations.

6. Which of the following is a supporting detail for the role of religion in Mayan life?
- A. Priests had significant authority and influenced state matters.
- B. Mayan farmers cultivated maize, beans, squash, and chili peppers.
- C. The Mayans invented papermaking and the compass.
- D. The Mayan government was a monarchy with a single ruler.

7. In the text, the word "zenith" most nearly means:
    o A. Lowest point
    o B. Middle stage
    o <u>C. Highest point</u>
    o D. Initial phase
8. Who is the author most likely to agree with regarding the interpretation of Mayan art?
    o A. An archaeologist who sees it purely as decorative
    o <u>B. A historian who perceives it as a symbolic representation of their culture</u>
    o C. A biologist who studies the ecological influences on art
    o D. An economist who focuses on the art's material value

Text 9

Annotation Checklist

As you read the text, please annotate it using the following checklist:

- ☑ Underline any main ideas
- ☑ Circle any words you don't know
- ☑ Look up the words online
- ☑ Reread anything you don't understand
- ☑ Summarize after rereading
- ☑ Write Down things you find interesting

yes!

Note Taking

Name: _____

Date: _____

The Mali Empire: An Epoch of Wealth and Wisdom

Introduction

In the annals of history, few empires in Africa have captured the imagination like the Mali Empire. This empire, which flourished from the 13th to the 16th centuries, was not just a political force but also a cultural and economic beacon in West Africa. Renowned for its wealth, extensive trade networks, and scholarly pursuits, the Mali Empire is a shining example of Africa's historical grandeur.

Located in the Sahel region, the empire encompassed parts of modern-day Mali, Senegal, Gambia, Guinea, Niger, Nigeria, Chad, and Mauritania. It was a melting pot of diverse African cultures, where bustling markets, grand mosques, and scholarly debates highlighted a sophisticated society.

History

The Mali Empire's story begins with the decline of the Ghana Empire, the previous regional power. Sundiata Keita, known as the Lion King, emerged from the small state of Niani to forge this new empire in the early 13th century. His victory at the Battle of Kirina in 1235 marked the beginning of Mali's ascendancy.

The empire's most celebrated ruler, Mansa Musa, ascended the throne in 1312. Under his reign, the empire reached unparalleled heights of wealth and territorial expansion. Mansa Musa is celebrated for his pilgrimage to Mecca in 1324, a journey that demonstrated Mali's wealth and pious devotion to the Islamic world. He established Timbuktu and Gao as crucial cultural and learning centers, attracting scholars, artists, and architects from across the Islamic world.

Post-Mansa Musa, the empire continued to prosper but gradually weakened due to internal strife and external pressures. The rise of the Songhai Empire and the Moroccan invasion in the 16th century marked the decline of Mali's dominance.

Government

The Mali Empire's governance was an intricate mix of centralized authority and local autonomy. The Mansa had supreme power, controlling military, economic, and judicial matters. The empire was divided into provinces, each overseen by a farba (governor), who was usually a member of the royal family or a trusted noble.

The Mansa's court, located in the capital Niani, was the empire's administrative and political heart. The court was composed of high-ranking officials and advisers, including the qadi (judges), finance ministers, and military commanders. This administrative apparatus allowed the empire to maintain control over its vast territories, ensuring stability and prosperity.

Religion

Islam's introduction into the Mali Empire through the trans-Saharan trade routes had a profound impact. The ruling class embraced Islam, which led to the construction of mosques and madrasas, particularly in cities like Timbuktu and Gao. These cities became centers of Islamic learning, attracting scholars from various parts of the Muslim world.

Despite the rulers' embrace of Islam, traditional African religious practices and beliefs remained influential among the general populace. This led to a syncretic blend of Islamic and indigenous practices, evident in the unique cultural expressions and rituals of the Malian people.

Cultural Flourishing and Education

The Mali Empire was not only a political and economic powerhouse but also a beacon of culture and learning. Under the patronage of Mansa Musa and other rulers, Timbuktu and other cities became centers of learning, attracting scholars, poets, and artists from across the Islamic world. The University of Sankore in Timbuktu was a renowned institution, its libraries filled with thousands of manuscripts on various subjects from theology to astronomy.

The empire's commitment to Islamic education did not overshadow its rich oral tradition. Griots, or storytellers, were custodians of oral history, using music and epic tales to preserve the empire's history and transmit cultural values. This tradition of storytelling and music is a cultural legacy that continues to influence West African art forms today.

Architectural and Scientific Achievements

Malian architecture from this period is exemplified by the construction of grand mosques made of mud-brick and wooden beams, such as the iconic Great Mosque of Djenné. These architectural marvels display a unique African-Islamic fusion and are celebrated for their intricate designs and sustainability.

In science, the scholars of Mali contributed to the fields of astronomy, medicine, and mathematics. The astronomical observations made in Mali were crucial for navigation and timekeeping, particularly in the context of the Islamic lunar calendar and prayer times.

Economic Diversification and Decline

While the Mali Empire's economy was initially bolstered by gold and salt trade, it eventually diversified into agriculture, with the Niger River valley providing fertile grounds for cultivation. This diversification, however, couldn't shield the empire from the economic shifts that came with the opening of new trade routes by European explorers along the West African coast.

The empire's decline was accelerated by internal political strife, with successive rulers unable to maintain the authority and unity that characterized the reigns of earlier Mansas. The rise of powerful regional leaders led to fragmentation, and the burgeoning Songhai Empire further challenged Mali's dominance.

Legacy and Historical Significance

The legacy of the Mali Empire in West Africa is profound. It laid the groundwork for subsequent empires in the region, such as the Songhai, and influenced the political, cultural, and economic landscape of West Africa.

The memory of the Mali Empire, particularly the reign of Mansa Musa, lives on as a symbol of African wealth and historical greatness. It challenges narratives that overlook Africa's rich contributions to world history and serves as a source of pride and inspiration for people of African descent globally.

Mali's history is a testament to the region's historical dynamism and its central role in global medieval trade and cultural exchanges. The architectural marvels, scholarly achievements, and rich oral traditions of the Mali Empire continue to be studied and admired, underscoring the importance of preserving and celebrating African history.

1 What event marked the beginning of the Mali Empire's ascendancy?
- A. The construction of the Great Mosque of Djenné
- B. The pilgrimage of Mansa Musa to Mecca
- C. Sundiata Keita's victory at the Battle of Kirina
- D. The establishment of the University of Sankore in Timbuktu

2. Which region did the Mali Empire NOT encompass?
- A. Nigeria
- B. Egypt
- C. Senegal
- D. Guinea

3. What was a major reason for the Mali Empire's decline in the 16th century?
- A. The spread of Christianity
- B. The rise of the Songhai Empire and foreign traders
- C. A devastating plague that swept through the empire
- D. A massive rebellion by the empire's peasants

4. Based on the text, what role did religion play in the Mali Empire?
- A. It was strictly limited to personal beliefs without influence on governance.
- B. Islam was embraced by the ruling class, leading to the establishment of educational and religious centers.
- C. Christianity overshadowed Islamic practices throughout the empire.
- D. Traditional African religious practices were completely replaced by Islam.

5. What is the main idea of the "Cultural Flourishing and Education" section?
- A. The Mali Empire was known for its rich oral traditions and music.
- B. Education and culture thrived in Mali, with cities like Timbuktu becoming centers of learning.
- C. The Mali Empire focused solely on military and economic advancements.
- D. The Mali Empire's culture was predominantly influenced by European cultures.

6. Which of the following is a supporting detail about the Mali Empire's economic diversification?
- A. The empire was known for its unique architectural styles.
- B. The Niger River valley was utilized for agricultural cultivation.
- C. The Mali Empire's economy was solely based on the gold trade.
- D. Scientific advancements were the main focus of the empire's economy.

7. In the context of the text, the word "syncretic" most likely means:
    - A. Conflicting or opposing
    - B. Combining different forms of belief or practice
    - C. Ancient or traditional
    - D. Scientific or technological
8. Who was Mansa Musa?
    - A. The founder of the Mali Empire
    - B. A governor in the Mali Empire
    - C. The most celebrated ruler of the Mali Empire
    - D. A famous scholar from the Mali Empire

9. How did the introduction of Islam influence the Mali Empire's cultural and educational development?

_____

_____

_____

_____

_____

_____

10. Discuss how the geographic location of the Mali Empire contributed to its economic prosperity.

_____

_____

_____

_____

_____

_____

11. Describe the administrative structure of the Mali Empire as outlined in the text.

_____

_____

_____

_____

_____

_____

Analyze the historical significance of the Mali Empire, focusing on its contributions to culture, education, and the close by countries. Use specific examples from the text to support your discussion.

_____
_____
_____
_____
_____
_____
_____
_____
_____
_____
_____
_____
_____
_____
_____
_____
_____
_____
_____
_____
_____
_____
_____
_____
_____
_____
_____
_____

Answer key

1 What event marked the beginning of the Mali Empire's ascendancy?
   - A. The construction of the Great Mosque of Djenné
   - B. The pilgrimage of Mansa Musa to Mecca
   - C. Sundiata Keita's victory at the Battle of Kirina
   - D. The establishment of the University of Sankore in Timbuktu
2. Which region did the Mali Empire NOT encompass?
   - A. Nigeria
   - B. Egypt
   - C. Senegal
   - D. Guinea
3. What was a major reason for the Mali Empire's decline in the 16th century?
   - A. The spread of Christianity
   - B. The rise of the Songhai Empire and foreign traders
   - C. A devastating plague that swept through the empire
   - D. A massive rebellion by the empire's peasants
4. Based on the text, what role did religion play in the Mali Empire?
   - A. It was strictly limited to personal beliefs without influence on governance.
   - B. Islam was embraced by the ruling class, leading to the establishment of educational and religious centers.
   - C. Christianity overshadowed Islamic practices throughout the empire.
   - D. Traditional African religious practices were completely replaced by Islam.
5. What is the main idea of the "Cultural Flourishing and Education" section?
   - A. The Mali Empire was known for its rich oral traditions and music.
   - B. Education and culture thrived in Mali, with cities like Timbuktu becoming centers of learning.
   - C. The Mali Empire focused solely on military and economic advancements.
   - D. The Mali Empire's culture was predominantly influenced by European cultures.
6. Which of the following is a supporting detail about the Mali Empire's economic diversification?
   - A. The empire was known for its unique architectural styles.
   - B. The Niger River valley was utilized for agricultural cultivation.
   - C. The Mali Empire's economy was solely based on the gold trade.
   - D. Scientific advancements were the main focus of the empire's economy.

7. In the context of the text, the word "syncretic" most likely means:
    - ○ A. Conflicting or opposing
    - ○ <u>B. Combining different forms of belief or practice</u>
    - ○ C. Ancient or traditional
    - ○ D. Scientific or technological
8. Who was Mansa Musa?
    - ○ A. The founder of the Mali Empire
    - ○ B. A governor in the Mali Empire
    - ○ <u>C. The most celebrated ruler of the Mali Empire</u>
    - ○ D. A famous scholar from the Mali Empire

Text 10

Annotation Checklist

As you read the text, please annotate it using the following checklist:

- ☑ Underline any main ideas
- ☑ Circle any words you don't know
- ☑ Look up the words online
- ☑ Reread anything you don't understand
- ☑ Summarize after rereading
- ☑ Write Down things you find interesting

yes!

Note Taking

The Mongol Empire: An Epic of Conquest and Integration

Introduction

Envision a vast expanse stretching from the steppes of Mongolia to the edges of Europe, an empire that redefined the course of history with its breathtaking conquests and unexpected unifications. This was the Mongol Empire, a realm forged by the vision and valor of Genghis Khan and his descendants. It was an empire that, at its zenith, was the largest contiguous land empire in human history, renowned not just for its military might but also for its intricate trade networks, cultural diversity, and diplomatic dexterity.

Comprehensive History

The origins of the Mongol Empire are rooted in the early 13th century, with the rise of Genghis Khan, born as Temujin. He united the disparate Mongolian tribes through a combination of diplomatic cunning and military might. In 1206, he was proclaimed Genghis Khan, meaning "universal ruler," marking the inception of the Mongol Empire.

Under Genghis Khan's leadership, the Mongols embarked on an era of rapid expansion. Their conquests were marked by innovative military strategies, unmatched horsemanship, and often-brutal tactics. The Mongols decimated the armies of larger but less mobile nations, capturing vast territories across Asia.

After Genghis Khan's death in 1227, his successors, including his sons and grandsons, continued the expansion. Ogedei Khan, his third son, expanded into Russia and Eastern Europe. Subsequent rulers pushed into the Middle East and the Song Dynasty of China. The establishment of the Yuan Dynasty in China by Kublai Khan in 1271 marked the peak of Mongol power.

The Mongol Empire facilitated a significant period of cultural and economic exchange between East and West. This era, often referred to as the "Pax Mongolica" or Mongol Peace, saw an unprecedented movement of goods, technologies, and ideas along the Silk Road. It was a time when a merchant or a diplomat could travel from one end of the empire to the other with relative safety and ease.

Government Structure and Administration

The governance of the Mongol Empire was characterized by a blend of military organization, meritocratic principles, and adaptability. Genghis Khan established a legal code, the Yassa, which governed everything from military discipline to civil affairs. He appointed governors and administrators based on merit and loyalty, often choosing talented individuals from the conquered populations.

Each region of the empire, known as a khanate, was ruled by a member of Genghis Khan's family. This system maintained a sense of unity while allowing for regional autonomy. The empire's administration borrowed heavily from the sophisticated bureaucratic systems of China and Persia, blending them with Mongolian traditions.

The Mongol Empire's governance was notable for its pragmatism and flexibility. The Mongols did not impose their culture or language on the conquered peoples. Instead, they adopted elements of the local administration, religion, and customs, which helped them manage the diverse empire effectively.

Religious Policies and Cultural Impact

The Mongols' approach to religion was marked by remarkable tolerance and inclusivity. Genghis Khan and his successors were shrewd in their understanding that religious tolerance was essential for governing a vast and culturally diverse empire. While the Mongols practiced Tengrism and Shamanism, they respected and protected all religions within their domain.

This policy of religious tolerance led to a thriving cultural and intellectual climate. Scholars, artists, and religious figures from various parts of the world were welcomed at the Mongol court. The empire became a melting pot of Islamic, Christian, Buddhist, and Confucian thought and traditions.

The transmission of knowledge and ideas across the empire laid the groundwork for advancements in science, art, and literature. The Mongol capital of Karakorum, for instance, became a center for artistic and intellectual exchange, hosting artists and scholars from across Eurasia.

Military Strategies and Conquests

The Mongol military was a formidable force, renowned for its discipline, mobility, and innovative tactics. Genghis Khan revolutionized Mongol warfare with his emphasis on mobility, intelligence gathering, and psychological warfare. The Mongol army was primarily composed of cavalry, both heavy and light, allowing for rapid movements across vast distances.

The Mongols employed a variety of tactics, including feigned retreats, encirclement, and the use of advanced siege technologies. Their ability to adapt to different environments and combat situations was unparalleled. The Mongol conquests were not only military campaigns but also exercises in psychological warfare, often instilling fear and awe in their adversaries.

Decline and Fragmentation

The decline of the Mongol Empire began in the late 13th century, following a series of unsuccessful military campaigns, most notably in Japan and Southeast Asia. The vastness of the empire made it increasingly difficult to govern effectively, leading to administrative challenges and internal strife.

After the death of Kublai Khan in 1294, the unity of the empire began to fray. The khanates, governed by different branches of Genghis Khan's family, started to operate more independently, often engaging in conflicts with each other. The Black Death further weakened the empire in the mid-14th century, disrupting trade and causing widespread mortality.

By the end of the 14th century, the Mongol Empire had fragmented into several smaller khanates, each pursuing its own path. The most notable successor states were the Yuan Dynasty in China, the Golden Horde in Russia, the Chagatai Khanate in Central Asia, and the Ilkhanate in Persia.

Legacy and Historical Significance

The legacy of the Mongol Empire is complex and multifaceted. On one hand, it was an empire built on conquest and often-brutal subjugation. On the other, it was an era of significant cultural exchange, economic prosperity, and intellectual advancement.

The Mongol Empire played a crucial role in shaping the geopolitical contours of Eurasia. It connected the East and the West, facilitating trade and cultural exchanges that had lasting impacts on the development of the world. The empire's influence can be seen in the spread of technologies, the transmission of ideas, and the blending of cultures across Asia and Europe.

In modern times, the Mongol Empire is often remembered for its military successes and the larger-than-life figure of Genghis Khan. However, its contributions to the cultural and economic development of the medieval world remain an enduring part of its legacy.

1 Who founded the Mongol Empire in the early 13th century
- A. Kublai Khan
- B. Ogedei Khan
- C. Genghis Khan
- D. Tamerlane

2. What was the "Yassa" in the context of the Mongol Empire?
- A. A religious text
- B. A military strategy
- C. A legal code
- D. A trade agreement

3. Which of the following regions was NOT conquered by the Mongol Empire?
- A. Russia and Eastern Europe
- B. The Middle East
- C. Japan
- D. The Song Dynasty of China

4. Based on the text, what was a significant factor in the decline of the Mongol Empire?
- A. The adoption of local customs and religions
- B. Successful military campaigns in Japan and Southeast Asia
- C. Internal strife and administrative challenges
- D. The establishment of the Yuan Dynasty in China

5. What is the main idea of the section titled "Religious Policies and Cultural Impact"?
- A. The Mongol Empire's military strategies were influenced by religious beliefs.
- B. The Mongols' religious tolerance led to a thriving cultural and intellectual climate.
- C. All religions were banned except for Tengrism and Shamanism.
- D. Religious conflicts were the primary cause of the empire's decline.

6. Which detail from the text supports the idea of the Mongol Empire facilitating cultural exchange?
- A. The empire's rapid expansion under Genghis Khan
- B. The use of advanced siege technologies in warfare
- C. The movement of goods, technologies, and ideas along the Silk Road during the Pax Mongolica
- D. The introduction of the legal code, the Yassa

7. In the context of the text, the term "khanate" most closely means:
   - ○ A. A military unit
   - ○ B. A religious doctrine
   - ○ C. A region or territory governed by a Khan
   - ○ D. A legal system
8. What was a key characteristic of the Mongol military?
   - ○ A. Primarily infantry-based tactics
   - ○ B. Heavy reliance on naval power
   - ○ C. Exceptional discipline and mobility with a focus on cavalry
   - ○ D. Use of gunpowder and firearms

9. How did Genghis Khan's approach to governance and culture influence the administration of the Mongol Empire?

_____

_____

_____

_____

_____

_____

10. Explain how the Mongol Empire's vastness contributed to its administrative challenges and eventual fragmentation.

_____

_____

_____

_____

_____

_____

11. Describe the impact of the Mongol Empire on the cultural and economic development of the medieval world, as outlined in the text.

_____

_____

_____

_____

_____

_____

Discuss the moral implications of the Mongol Empire. Were they, in the long run, a force for progress or evil?

_____
_____
_____
_____
_____
_____
_____
_____
_____
_____
_____
_____
_____
_____
_____
_____
_____
_____
_____
_____
_____
_____
_____
_____
_____
_____
_____
_____
_____

Answer key

1 Who founded the Mongol Empire in the early 13th century
   - A. Kublai Khan
   - B. Ogedei Khan
   - C. Genghis Khan
   - D. Tamerlane

2. What was the "Yassa" in the context of the Mongol Empire?
   - A. A religious text
   - B. A military strategy
   - C. A legal code
   - D. A trade agreement

3. Which of the following regions was NOT conquered by the Mongol Empire?
   - A. Russia and Eastern Europe
   - B. The Middle East
   - C. Japan
   - D. The Song Dynasty of China

4. Based on the text, what was a significant factor in the decline of the Mongol Empire?
   - A. The adoption of local customs and religions
   - B. Successful military campaigns in Japan and Southeast Asia
   - C. Internal strife and administrative challenges
   - D. The establishment of the Yuan Dynasty in China

5. What is the main idea of the section titled "Religious Policies and Cultural Impact"?
   - A. The Mongol Empire's military strategies were influenced by religious beliefs.
   - B. The Mongols' religious tolerance led to a thriving cultural and intellectual climate.
   - C. All religions were banned except for Tengrism and Shamanism.
   - D. Religious conflicts were the primary cause of the empire's decline.

6. Which detail from the text supports the idea of the Mongol Empire facilitating cultural exchange?
   - A. The empire's rapid expansion under Genghis Khan
   - B. The use of advanced siege technologies in warfare
   - C. The movement of goods, technologies, and ideas along the Silk Road during the Pax Mongolica
   - D. The introduction of the legal code, the Yassa

7. In the context of the text, the term "khanate" most closely means:
    - o A. A military unit
    - o B. A religious doctrine
    - o C. A region or territory governed by a Khan
    - o D. A legal system
8. What was a key characteristic of the Mongol military?
    - o A. Primarily infantry-based tactics
    - o B. Heavy reliance on naval power
    - o C. Exceptional discipline and mobility with a focus on cavalry
    - o D. Use of gunpowder and firearms

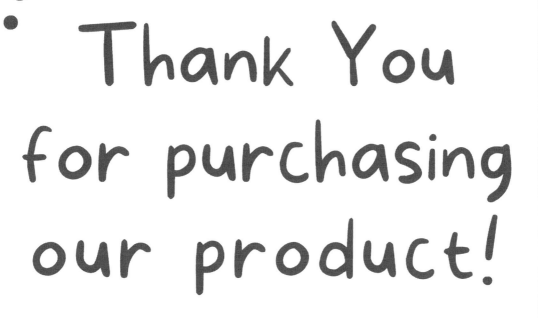

Thank You for purchasing our product!

If you would like a free gift and to join our newsletter, please email:

buddingbrainsbooksllc@gmail.com

Made in the USA
Las Vegas, NV
15 October 2024

96846673R00074